MW00790371

THIS IS A BLACKCURRANT PRESS PUBLICATION

INTO MY ROTATION - A COLLECTION OF SCRIBES

Written by Nolan P. Holloway, Jr.
Edited by Fran Issac

ISBN # 978-0-9840379-3-3

Printed in the United States of America
June 2012

FIRST EDITION

BLACK CURRANT
PRESS
www.blackcurrantpress.com

www.blackcurrantpress.com

MANTRA

The Spirit is my guide
Christ is my mark
GOD is my strength

INTO

MY

ROTATION

A COLLECTION OF

scribes

WRITTEN BY

NOLAN P. HOLLOWAY, JR.

TABLE OF CONTENTS

1st

ROTATION

Spiritual

A DIFFERENT KIND OF PARTY

We can party when two or more are gathered
Praise says "Let's get this party started"
The minister staff spins and mixes the spiritual groove to hype the crowd
Praise gets on the mic to MC
People sitting in the pews sipping on some Word

Some are on the floor doing the "Holy Dance"
Folks shout out to each other
The feeling is a Godly party mood

Joy and Happiness show up and get in on the fun
They go out in the crowd and motion to get people on the dance floor
When Praise raises the roof, Blessing comes down to keep the party
going
The house is live with the spirit of jubilation
Young and Old can "get down" and be part of the celebration

Pastor extends an invitation to join the club
"Anyone witnessing this gathering, Join Us"
A few step up and say they want to be in the midst
Everyone rejoices that we have new members joining our heavenly crew
We are now in preparation for the real invitation to

"The Eternal After Party"
***"With gladness and rejoicing shall they be brought: they shall enter
into the King's palace" Psalms 45:15***

BATTLE FOR ME
(Senryu style)

Fighting for my soul

The enemy is so strong

Look above for help

He will intercede

Feels like I'm losing my hold

The dark one wants me

I need to fight on

Hold on to the Light for strength

My soul is the prize

COMPILATION OF CLOUD WATCHING

Gliding slowly across an iridescent ceiling

A light has been left burning

Purposeful patience strolls to a heavenly destination

Power in the design - love in its color

Perfect contrast to fashion a mood

Transfigured in the vortex of imagination

All in the same room - each interpretation unique and valued

Understanding permeates the physical

Watching, emotionally connected

Essence of purity

DARKSIDE SEDUCTION

Is there a reason why the
darkness fascinates
Starry skies of peace give
falseness to the happenings
in the spaces below
Secret deals being negotiated
as if it will never be challenged
by the Light
Convincing ourselves that we
can chill with the night
Hanging out with the shadows
to sooth our troubled souls
Some rationalize to ease the
pain but remain cool with the
darkness
The actions and energy of people
combine to awake the night
from its sleep into awareness
Even I am drawn to its beckoning
me to venture out to play for awhile
But there is a Light in me that guides
away from what can destroy
The night darkness is alluring and
seductive
Values and morals metemorphosize
into a new and dangerous mindset
Humans-old and young wrap
themselves in the darkness of
night
Becoming what they truly are not
Hiding beyond and behind the
Cover of Darkness
The darkness can be tamed by
balancing it with the Light
So many are consumed by the
darkness of night
Souls may be forfeited if the Light
never intercedes
Your inner Light must shine to see

and be seen

DRY BONES

Pieces of my past forms my present
Some of these keep me from my full
happiness in this life given
These bones are dead, heavy and make
me so weary

Believed that I had shed them but alas
events' now living shows that I have not
So this day a new challenge lies before me
Prophesy and make these dry bones "live"
Face the past and cast nebulous memories and
deeds into the "sea of forgetfulness"

Now emerging from the valley of dry bones
with hope and full of new-found power
To feed me with the hope for blessings for me
and people within my life circle
The power to speak my destiny to life eternal
From the One who breathed universal essence into these
"Dry Bones"

FORGOT TO REMEMBER

Memories fade into the recesses
of my mind

Some beautiful -
Orchestra of trees and flowers
swaying in the daily breeze
Smells of honeysuckle fills my nostrils
on an afternoon stroll
Sounds of birds chirping, insects buzzing and
creatures scurrying about
Traffic rolling thru underneath a brightly lit
sky
forgot to remember

Children playing, laughter and the innocence
they share
Smiles on passerby's faces I encounter en route to
my destination

forgot to remember

People I have known in my lifetime
that had a profound influence on who I have become
at this very moment
Sharing excitement of life – good times

forgot to remember

Words that were spoken by my parents, seniors
and extended family
Bits of conversations with acquaintances and strangers
buried deep in my subconscious mind

forgot to remember

Some painful -
Loss of friends and relationships
Λ setting sun never to rise again
Falling off the path to happiness and prosperity
by the decisions I made – allowed my control

to be handed over to the enemy
No clue that I was being manipulated by the
forces of darkness
Giving me the excuses to justify my sins
Leading my ear to real and imaginary "voices"
what I thought were reason
Caught in a web of lies and deceit

forgot to remember

Serving my own needs with the selfishness of a rich man
clinging to his wealth
Unfinished conversations to rectify my filthy rags
Actions I cannot take back like past days gone by
never to be recaptured
Reaching out only to be ignored or rejected

forgot to remember

Shackled by the chains of my misdeeds
Self punished in the prison of my own making
– struggling just to get thru each day

I Forgot the most important aspect
that I need to Remember
Forgot because of doing my "own thing"
The outcome was
wasted time
personal damage
self depression
from a deep hole that I cried out of

He never forgot to remember
And because of that
I am redeemed

FRUITFUL TREE

As a seed I was planted
Two joining into one to form me
Nurtured to grow upward-outward
Moving toward the tree I would be

The two mature ones gave me shade
Protected from the elements the tree they made

Two more were sown to complete the family
Watchfully nourished and watered
Uprooted and planted to our new home
A community that was ordered

But the father tree dominated the land
Wouldn't allow us to grow and make a stand

Determined to make a way on my own
To move out of the shadow of the one
Extending in a different direction to feel a different soil
Making my limbs grow anxious and run

Plenty of sun to gain the light of knowledge
Wandered onto the dark road to wreckage

Weathered storms and choking weeds
Beat down with the weight of life
Entangled in the struggle
Hard on myself with guilt and strife

A plan was always in place for this seed
To help other trees in need

It is now the season to bear fruit
Words and actions bring all to light
Living, being, growing, doing
What is honorable and right

So I choose to now become that fruit tree
I somehow knew, it was always a part of me

GIVEN

Easy to be about self
Existing in a world of our making
Absorbed in what we deem as important and
meaningful
Playing god as to how we live and breathe in our existence
Like an emperor who can turn thumbs down
to sentence death to anyone we choose with no
remorse or thought
Many of us live in these "worlds" made real by
what and how our thinking takes shape
Not caring about anything but us
Planets revolving around "me"
But we have been given something that will make
meaning of our world and brighten the life we live
It is called "Given"
Given life from the womb
Given redemption by the Almighty Father
Given a choice to how we choose to live
The title of this scribe is "Given"
Simply by giving we gain the freedom
to move outside our world to the vast universe
of our fellow beings

Male

Female

Young

Old
What would we do with this gift
Waste it on ourselves or make it
so rich and fulfilling to move to a
World of "Given"

GOING HOME

One day we will return home.
Why are you thinking it is where you live?
A place fixed in your daily rotation.
Decorated with the accumulation of inanimate objects.
Your personal sanctuary from the world on the other side
Of the walls of the abode.

Home is layered in relativity.
For some expansive space that cannot be occupied all the
time.
For most it is modest and gives comfort to the body.
Conditions on the scale of the clinical cleanliness to landfill
dirty.
To others it is wherever they happen to be at that moment.

But going home to me is the separation of the body from the
spirit.
Some that I have heard about and known — have gone
home.
The body to return to the earth and the spirit...............
So the contemplation question will be
When you go home – where will it be?

In the Midst of thought

In the midst of thought
Of the price that was wrought
Of the holiday season
That gives us reason
To reflect on its meaning
Society makes so demeaning
The significance of this time of year
A child was born with anticipation and cheer
Fulfilling prophecy of old
To a world turned bitter and cold
Bringing hope for redemption
After the first temptation
So innocent and humble was His birth
In simple clothes He was girthed
Heaven and earth celebrated His coming
Because of the second chance of becoming
His children once again
So be mindful and begin
To live in harmony and grace.

JOY FOR ME

It is a blessing for me to still be on this journey
Juxtaposition against the Universal Time it is a short one
So many have gone on to an alternate reality
My belief gives me the knowledge of where this all leads to
So many paths are laid before us to choose
Where do we go and why follow?
Questions that will surely outlive me, no doubt
I have chosen to search for the right path to follow
The end will be glorious, but I must ready myself
A guide has been given to all of us

The knowledge is so easy to obtain but the
application is so difficult to apply
In order to find Joy, I must follow the true path
Can't convince everyone to join, for true Joy
is found when I receive it and can share with others
The importance of that fact enraptures me
The dark flow is ever present to rob me of the Joy
that I deserve

Many times I allow it to control and consume me
By doubting
who
what
and whom I belong to
Must maintain sight of that
It's so easy to become distracted and worn down
I so desire to embrace the fullness of Joy in my Life
Perhaps I'm searching in the wrong place
Emanating the wrong energy
On my daily walk thru this life, I will
strive
reach
will
Myself to obtain Joy and keep it close to my
Heart

Place where we are

A pounding gavel makes my head ache
and awakens me to the reality that we have
moved to this place where we are

I have fought myself in the ring of circumstance
to determine if I stay aggressive or move with
purpose of strategy

Looking behind our footprints have disappeared
Can see the path but the sites passed are muddled
with worrying about what lies ahead

Time sitting in the grass by the edge of the path
resting but always ready to move
Memories blow at various speeds to cool or just
whisper on what might be on the horizon

Place where we are tingles with rightness
revealing that chance does not belong
We are surrounded by ones that have been asked to
be at the place where we are

Leaning against the tree of patience, inhaling the air
of love and touching your smile with my fingers
Gives me joy to continue our journey to the
place where we are

MY THINKING
(Of thoughts In Him)

My attempt to contemplate
The thoughts of Jesus
Is like grasping how the universe was created
Too limited and feeble am I
God and the Son as One
Son in the flesh of man
Sharing the burdens that comes with this imperfect vessel
because of our past transgression
Forty days and nights He fasted
and was tempted by Satan
He thought of the Father
To give Him strength and fortitude
to endure
A task we could not fathom to achieve
Feeling hunger, fatigue and pain
His thinking of the limitations in the body
Having knowledge of the Power He possessed
Thoughts of a prophecy that needed
to be fulfilled
In the garden praying and thinking of what He
was about to face
Fear, trepidation, nervousness may have been
going on in His mind
Possible frustration with us but
knowing how we think - willing to sacrifice
Himself for us with clarity and purpose to please the
Father
It humbles me to force my thinking
to how His mind was, is and will be
Grace and mercy is what I feel
The conclusion is that the thoughts
of Jesus stayed focused and pointed
to the Father at all times
My desire and yours should be the
same................

PRECIOUS SOUL
(Lives in my house)

Living in this flesh-dwelling in this house that breathes
My soul resides within
Am I Soul or Body?
My house is not made to last forever
One day to be condemned and torn down
For my Soul I will have moved
Will your soul have a new home?
Or be homeless when death arrives to evict
Having to live in hell's shelter for eternity
Not taking care of the "home" you have been
given while you are on this side
House being empty because you believe
no one lives inside
The house is "you" with nothing inside
Is your Soul precious?
Having an empty house with nothing to
cherish or preserve means no
My Soul is precious to the One that formed me
Fortified my home because of the strength
given to my Soul making it the owner of this
house
So that one day it will be prepared to live anew
Will your Soul be taken for granted?
Existing to go nowhere
Living by your desires-knowing that the
Soul you are given will die from thirst for the truth
Precious Soul
Graced freely from the heavens
Live through your Soul and not the body
For the body is the house that will surely perish
But to live thru the Soul and one day
you will live in your mansion for
eternity

PURPOSEFUL PEACE

Blessed be another day
of life that I have been given
Breathing breathe gifted to
me from a power beyond my
understanding
My mind clouded with worldly things
A minefield of explosive situations
of my own creation
Disturbed sleep of thoughts taken from
the day
Natural and supernatural
Driven by me and coerced by the one
whose purpose is dark

But this day I walk boldly and with direction
New air of life I inhale into my lungs
Filled with freshness and divine Power
My purpose is forming before me
Guiding and directing
I take my next gift with a humbling reverence

Those I loved disappoint
I now understand that a choice that I must
make to do and be in purposeful peace
To make my mind clean and pure
before I go to rest
Seeking peace upward and within

REACHING OUT

I NEED YOU RIGHT NOW
Keep control of myself I vow

THE MOMENT IS HERE
I want you near

So I'm reaching out to get what I need from you
To shake off this feeling blue

But when reached, the space was void
I became frozen like a mindless droid

This is when I want help with those tough times
Keeping my mind from sinful crimes

But I would be better off reaching upward
Stretching toward

The Heavens that hold the answers to my dilemma
Now I see a glimmer

Of hope, connection and the answers I have been seeking
The air clears, not with the rancid smell reeking

Of dirty, foul and impure consciousness
But the joy of His wholeness

So instead of reaching out
Better to reach up
Rather than out
You will never be disappointed

SHAKEN FAITH

Written to wherever you are presently
We believe and hope – holding on to faith of better ones and times
Folks truly disappoint – can't see clearly thru the tears
Could be your sight thru the mental glasses you wear
Stiff life winds blow the branches off our limbs
Swaying under its force – some creaking, cracking and others breaking
Blight eats away at our skin – discolored and disheartening to gaze upon
Shaken faith
Having knowledge of the path to strength – so difficult to grasp and pull close
Do you love yourself?
It's so easy when the sky is blue and the sun smiles its brilliant radiance
But this day is overcast with doubt and fear of what is and beyond
A need to navigate past flesh and rise to Spirit – the smoke from our inner
selves rising to the heavens
Shaken faith
Muddle through the temporary condition
So hard and draining – cannot surrender when despair feels like a friend
Looking for a hand to reach out and –
Shake the faith back into us

SUNDAY MOTHERS

Slowly they make their way into the sanctuary with a purpose to uplift and praise the Lord. It is time to worship - they move with patience and determination to the appointed place

GODLY

Silent wisdom is etched on the countenances revealing the strength of character each one processes

Members greet them one by one - they sit regally in the pews like queens holding court "Hello Mother" as they are greeted by the subjects giving admiration

EXISTENCE

Women of faith who grace us with their steadfast presence - dedicated to the uplifting the congregation

CHRIST

They are the very breathe in which the Spirit flows throughout the service Alone standing in the absence of men in their lives. The Church is now the family Leaning to higher Power to sustain the life force

GRACE

Giving love and guidance – rewarded with respect for the time dedicated to giving of themselves to seeing the vision become reality

The leader of the flock understands the importance of these women as the heart – the energy that pumps the life blood which drives the Body and makes it move Love emanates from the smiles when a familiar faces appears – it encompasses and moves within – motivates to emulate......

SUNRISE SERVICE

truly significant is this day
for if it never happened we would forever be lost

purposeful meaning for the chosen ones who will understand
and embrace its meaning
providing the key to unlocking the door of blessings to
give us the life that Christ desires for us

beginning in the darkness and ending in the glory of the
morning
perfect symmetry with our Lord in the dark tomb and rising
with ALL Power by sunrise on the third day

reflections on the price that was paid and the trueness of
prophecy fulfilled
sins condemned us to everlasting damnation – through His
crucifixion we are redeemed

as our lives have meaning – we serve and give praise during
this special service
having one mind allowing the Spirit to have his way

not aimlessly wandering thru, with no purpose of existence
sheep under the direction on Our Shepherd – who watches
over and protects us

we now have direction for ourselves by reaching out and
living through the spirit of His message
the law has been written on our hearts

heartfelt anticipation of this day brings tears and joy
intertwined
tears knowing where we were and how His act of Grace and
Mercy brings us to the joy of knowing we have a place in His
kingdom

coming together to celebrate the act for the salvation of
humankind
common bonds of sister and brotherhood

how important we are to Him - the sacrifice that was made for
us
to honor and remember the Rising of the Son

THANK YOU FATHER

When I think of the many things that you have done
Things I knew I didn't deserve
In the time of my youth

I did not understand why I served you as my Father
But the one I was given did things I could not believe
he took care of my basic needs
But never gave me the love or approval that I wanted
to hear from him

I asked you why things could be different
I loved and obeyed and did everything you asked of me
And thoughts went to dark places at times to question you
Father

But though this life and coming back to you things have become
clearer to me
Years I spent being angry and lashing out blaming my father for
the wrong in my life

My father came thru at times that surprised me
But my Father never left my side
Took me years and pain and living life to bring me the maturity I
needed to appreciate my father and come back to the harmony of
the Father

Thank you Father for your Grace and Mercy
And the opportunity to begin to Understand

THE ANATOMY OF THANKFULNESS

In a circle it flows
From within, outward to destinations
known and unknown
To return at a time unexpected
Therein lies the beauty of this body
which comes from each of us
Intentions drive this vehicle
A taxi to pick up and drop off passengers
thru the years
Faces vaguely familiar come and go
Goodness wells up and overflows
Caressing the face of forgiveness
Hate and ignorance speak vileness and
spew its poison darts of wickedness
But it quickly dissolved in wave of thankfulness
from distant shores
A shield to be taken into battle-hard as steel
but as soft as the look of love in the brightness of the day
Taken apart it stays together-freely dispersed
Never understanding how it is to return-but it really
doesn't matter
For the unity of this emotion transcends beyond death
to infinite planes to where our souls reside

THE ENEMY NEVER RESTS

Please guard your hopes with your very life
The enemy never rests
When riding the wave of good that I feel
when life is peaking
Then that subtle feeling - something is not
quite right
Somehow the light is not deserved
That being in darkness is where I should be placed
Moments flip upside down to wrongness
Happiness flees and passion morphs into anger
Why is this time reversing to sadness and cynicism?
I crave the fullness of the soul – flowing from that energy
that makes me want to live
The enemy never rests
Stirring up situations to steal and rob
my joy and everything that I hold close
Twisting and manipulating to make me hazy and blue
Attacking when I'm awake or asleep
It desires to destroy my very soul
with lies and deceit
My uplifting time is thrust downward
A weight crushing my spirit
The enemy never rests
Digging deep inside I search find a peace and
calm that surpasses all my understanding
A certain knowledge that everything is going to be
resolved and made right
My soul is lifted even in the face of what the
enemy may have plotted against me
The enemy never rests
And I will not rest for the enemy is ever present
My weapons will be prepared to face –
The enemy
Peace, truth and fortitude will keep me, my soul
and my faith intact
For as long as I believe........because
The enemy never rests

THE POWER

We have tapped into a special place
Two people different but on the same path
The Man
The women
Seeking to control the power of their lives
And the Power in their life
Together nothing is impossible
Our minds blend into one
We see hear speak on the same level
The feeling is surreal
The air is electric
Reconnect
Mental Vibe
Mutual attraction
To the Power on both levels
We have started a journey that will strengthen
our
Spirit
And enhance our love for the Power and each
other

THE WALK

The act is so simple
We take it for granted
It is not the physical act
But one that transcends the physical plane
Many of us perform this alone
Never with the realization that there is someone
Who
Wants to share in this
The Walk
Our minds must be in tune
To begin this
Our wills we must submit
But
By submitting ourselves
It frees us to take this Walk
For it is The Walk
In the Sprit

DESTINATION

on knees with head bowed
feeling defeated but looking upward
you see a battle is being engaged
layered on levels natural and super-natural
looking at what is facing your sight is hidden
seeing blindness which doesn't resonate
trusting in touch-other senses dulled by
the life grind
enslaved inside-bound outwardly
limited and ignorant
imprisoned in futility
stuck in the mud of the past with no hope
of ever moving forward
how is the escape to be made?
careful planning over time might hold
the key
touching the door there is no lock
so how does one gain freedom
from this earthly prison
hell is here-walking among us
devouring what it will
dominion it has been given in this world
recruiting ones that have lost their way
deceiving and stealing souls to sell
chains wrapped in the fullness of pleasure
choice masks handed out to the masses
the party is just beginning
a few will choose to make their trip
on an endless vacation-on the spirit
airline to a luxury resort-
on the isle of peace and prosperity

We Are Still Standing In Spite Of It All

We all have a potential to serve
Everyday new opportunities are laid before us

Allow your mind to be open to hearing His voice
Rise every morning with praise on your lips
Elevate your thoughts to a higher plane

Strength is needed to handle the trials of this world
Time is not something we can depend
Invite people to join in your worship experience
Love your enemies
Look and examine inwardly - for truth

Satan will attempt to destroy
Temptation will beckon you to take backward steps
Allow the Spirit to lead
Now is the time to take control
Do what is right even though noone else will
Into the Word people need to be
Never despair - look to the hills from whence help comes
Go to The Word for the knowledge that you seek

Investigate to know all the things that will lead to the truth
Never follow blindly - pray for guidance

Suffering is part of what the journey is - learn from it
Prepare yourself for what is to come
Invest in the reading and application of the Scriptures
Trust in the Lord - He will never forsake you
Enjoy the simple things and be grateful

Offer yourself to help others
Foster friendships that will last

Instruct and mentor our young people
Take time to tell someone you love them

Always be open to new challenges
Lean not on your own understanding - it ends badly
Love the Lord with all your heart, mind, and soul - love
your neighbor as yourself

WHEN TIME CALLS
(Tribute to Mother Fowler)

Smile that invites the Spirit into our midst
Speaking praises and carrying songs to uplift His Name
Conversations focused on the goodness of God
Gifts shared with all-sweet tasting and delicious
Lived history thru service to her Lord and family
The Father has now whispered that it is time for her to
come
home
In the care of angels she is
Peaceful in sleep until we one day join together in the
clouds
We love and miss you so mother
A place of honor has been kept for this appointed time
Full of the faith and companionship for us to keep seeking
the place
upon the hill where peace and refuge reside
You seeked and have found your way home
Tarried with us awhile to bring the knowledge of years past
Taking what we have gleaned to enrich the mind and warm
the
Heart
Farewell

2nd

ROTATION

Introspective

A ROTATIONAL MOMENT

In my shell humbled and exposed
Long I have thought of you two
Years passed as the grass grows in a yard
left abandoned and neglected

Never was my intent to leave it so
Actions speak to the character of me
Long time learning and listening to the
quiet voice of reason

Had to learn to be with me and educate
myself to who I am
Choices and complication clouded and
obscured me reaching out to you both

Thoughts and tears of lost moments and
what could have been
Now I stand somewhat bent but never
broken

Hope was never lost as the day when we
will unite in love questions
To fill in the voids that exists between all of
us

Water fills the dry pond so life can begin anew
Grateful and truly thankful that forgiveness
is possible and lives

So I say to you and your sister
Words have many meanings and I choose
carefully

Walking with Spirit given to me I want to
stroll and be with you
on the life road that has been laid before
me
Speaking power to what has rocked my soul

Being with both of you again............

BLUE'S IN D MINOR

Equilibrium off center

Pulling to one side

Not quite sure what it is

Wrongness stabs at the happiness

Something is amiss

Nagging is attempting to seduce psyche

Negative influences hanging on the street corner

Selling the drug of indifference

Smoke rising from the pipe

Lit in a dirty room of hopeleness

Stuck in the "high" place

Oblivious to reality - communing with evil

Sadness in the temple

Loss of possibilities of what could be

Walking dead - spirit with no soul

Faces with empty expressions

Zoned in on the negative key

Minus life - existence to blackness

Slaves to work the dark's one warehouse

Minor keys flow to tears - ceaseless sobbing

Cannot change - fixed in the minor key

A new song can be written - uplifting harmony

calming the mind and healing the heart

devalued to NONE

perception is in essence whatever one chooses
for it to be in the mind
important to one
irrelevant to another
how is value added without stripping thoughts naked?
humiliating
exposed
mocking hope
we all have the right to question the clarity of vision
explode to a larger view
fundamental freedom should be shared by everyone
but history's memories reminds that devaluation based on
perception
is whatever the one who rules wants
who has the power to feel the need to recognize only
themselves
moving to the sameness of circumstances
resting on the perceived
foundation of skewed righteousness of selfish beliefs
the voices of whom they deem inferior is silenced in the
endless chatter of prejudice
so hear and don't dismiss the cries of the devalued
for one day in their place you may be

EYES OPEN

This dichotomy is my world
Mind's eye shut then opened
Should I control the outcome of
My destiny
People love me with agape love
Full as a cornucopia
At a tasty and filling feast
For me to indulge to satisfy my desire
I'm mesmerized by how
Colorful and real this place can
Be
Happy thoughts and joy dominate
As the movement of ideas flow
Effortlessly
Thoroughly, am I understood?
Heard with clarity of ringing bells
Clear
Truly this is the world where I choose
To reside
Then
My eyes open
The real world appears
And is thrust upon me
No time to prepare
Everyone has a different attitude
Speaking I surmise clearly but
Not heard
Hearing the spoken words that
I have no cognitive evidence of

Uttering
Confusion, miscommunication has their
Way in ruling this physical domain
Happiness, joy being sucked out and
Dispatched to a place unreachable
I live thru my open eyes
Debating, compromising, devalued
For others enjoyment
I want to do what is right
Moving in step with the Word to apply
To this world
He gives peace to eyes closed to rest
I have a new found energy as the Spirit walks with me
Eyes open

FOUL

Surrounded by dark and dankness
Nothing to light the way at the moment
Senses under attack to the minuscule molecule
Looking overhead see the foul
Inhaling, smelling it too
Musty, swampy fog wisps up from the barren earth
At the brink, not daring to take another breath
Right at the time between something stirs within
An external predicament that cannot be controlled within
you
Reaching, grasping at the wind to kill the foul and birth
freshness
Feels good, brings tears to my mind, an inward cry to
cleanse the
foul within

Will your feet be struck in the mud of despair and
foreboding?
Hope thru the will that this will pass, other senses
to rise up and give
what is needed to banish this foulness of mind
and body to a place where it
is impotent, no power to influence

So breathe in the fragrance of sweetness of light
and air after the storm
Allow the foulness to dissolve and be consumed by the
purity of the

Soul

Full Circle

Situations come to fruition
The words run thru me as
lightning striking the earth
Air is frying and smoking
Cooking my mind

You have made a turn to close
this open circle
It was broken and unresolved
I lacked the understanding and
reasoning to feel what was occurring

But thru time and space our separation
has again been connected thru chance
An utterance I dared not think my ears
would ever receive

This circle is one of many touching my life
Full Circle gives me a consciousness to
embrace and cling onto the possibilities
of whatever
situations that create broken or a

Full Circle

GRINDING

granules fill my mouth
tastes like metal filings
cold and sharp
cutting into my tongue
ready to spew like knives at the next person
who approaches me
watching folks grind their words on
the stone to make them feel significant
I attempt to grind with them to no avail
so much noise from the perspective of
these folks sharpening their tools
heat from the friction on the wheel
burning my feelings
got me responding to them in the same way
sharpening my words to strike back
caught up in the spinning of the wheel
sound of metal against stone blasting at my ears
feeling that our words are finely crafted weapons
but are only awkwardly blunt instruments
with thought and preparation I'll
use my stone to form my words to a
razor shape edge
to cut with deeper meaning to
penetrate thru skin to bone
a surgical strike to cut away the harshness
and hate
that grinding inevitably causes
but to resonate with an understanding
that goes beyond the dull "grind"

I CHOOSE TO STAND

Been moving around for a minute
Dashing here and there
So many situations-curiously pulling at me

Light shining on many destinations
Moving causes loss
So I'm choosing to Stand
Still as a rock

Utilizing energy and wisdom within the earth
Focusing on that part of the Heavens that
flow across the star lit sky while I Stand and watch

Standing brings me clarity
intensified sight and a calming peace
Strength is a foundation that is
immovable as it resonates with true power

For this reason when life gets convoluted
I Choose to Stand

I CRY OUT (FOR UNDERSTANDING)

Silence like death fills the void that grows between us like a
disease
I utter my feelings, to me as clear as a quiet pond
A rock is dropped and disrupts and confuses the stillness
I cry out
At that precise moment, I know what is needed
But silence is all that I hear
Water and soil is required for growth
Without each being joined, nothing
I cry out
To be heard and understood at that moment
But it flees and disappears into the darkness of what we
don't comprehend
I cry out
But you don't hear
Feels like I'm all alone in a crowded room
Why are my words jumbled and maimed so when
I cry out
the understanding is murdered by deadly silence

JAZZNESS - FILL MY RESTLESS MIND

The horns gush back and forth like the sea rushing toward
the beach
and resonate throughout my body
Background sounds of silky violins and gentle guitars fills
the rest
Perfect symmetry of hearing and soulful feeling
My head slowly rolls to a subtle rhythm that
moves like the ocean in the afternoon

In tune with the color of sunset - soft but powerful orange,
kissed by red , and breathe on by blue
The piano joins like birds chirping with rising crescendo as
the day turns to twilight, then evening
Waves crash against the rocks as a thundering bass
The stars turn on as subtle lights in the outdoor jazz club
Swaying trees ask the short bushes for a dance
But they are already moving as the breeze
encourages them to
join together
There is a peace as this enters my mind
Visions that are felt and not seen with eyesight
But with eyes of the soul and mind that is the
Jazzness

That is the magic and spirit of these sounds that when
combined bring completeness to my being
A spring of goodness wells up in me
soothing and tingling inside

My restless mind leans back and beckons for a taste to
quench my thirst for the Jazzness
At that moment I am filled and content because of the
fullness
and beauty that comes together at that precise moment
which electrifies with the luminance of bright sea creatures

As the music fades into silence; I can still feel the residual
vibrations
moving my soul to peace...............................

LIFE MOVES

A decision made to come
back home
Needed movement in the right direction
My earthly father is no longer
here to bridge the space of my
understanding
But by Glory a man has provided guidance
and direction
A newness of Spirit to know
of truth and how it blesses the lives he touches
my Life Moves as the perception I have changes and
grows
Life moves toward the anointing of a man
appointed by God
He toils to lead toward the vision given by the
Most High
my life has been influenced by his flow
Lessons of life
Wisdom to deal with the daily trials and
victories-great and small
He has said look to the hills from where
Help comes
Knowing him has been an affirmation
to me
This scribe is to articulate how his passion,
humor and insight has made
My
Life
Move

MEANING BECOMING CLEAR

Through it all I question myself
But no need if He is in control
In the midst of our heated exchanges
A voice tells me if I am wrong
Gives me mission to make it right
or my spirit will be out of balance
Moments sometimes overwhelm
Wave on top of wave of misfortune
Making me feel I'm destroyed
Even when I know I'm not
The enemy is cunning-he clouds my
thoughts and wraps me in despair
Creates mirages of what he wants me
to see
So to my knees I must go
Not to submit to the enemy-but to show
reverence to the One most high
Low to be made high
My Spirit rises when I focus on the Goodness
He fills me with and I know that you and I
will be together
I may not be able to see it
But thru prayer and faith
He sees and knows

MINDFUL

Mindful of my mortality
Ultimately rules over my inner sanctum
Time is destined to stop for me
As the seconds grow up into years, will I be thought of?
Clocks will continue to tick when I'm gone
As I move thru time the more I am conscious of this
Tangled reality becomes unraveled, making me mindful of my life
Emptying thoughts that are truly not important
Need to change my relative mind focus
to flow outside and beyond where I am
To be mindful of who I am
Wasting time being mindless and not mindful
of what my purpose is
Like a room with no light and sound
Physically moving but mentally stagnant
Stale and stuck like ignored food in the frig
Appears fresh but a closer look reveals rot and mold
Cycling thru the life circle coming back to the center
Merging mindfulness and body into oneness like the sky bending into the horizon
Transitioning spirit moving in a physical realm
Mindful of the finality of this vessel I live in but
knowing that I'm pushing my force outward,
I can feel, love and pull others into my thoughts
Forever applies to those who believe as I
 of something beyond this experience on earth
Moving forward as a streaking comet I will leave
a trail that will be seen by many to remember that
I was here

MUSIC IS MY ROTATION

Spending my day with my ears plugged in
sound enters, my nerves ignite, my mind surges
Visuals I can see when my eyes are open
jamming with the band - playing all the sounds
that fill my ears
Taking me to that magical mind paradise
escaping inward to a alternate existence
Lost in the sounds
gravitating outside reality into elements that can be
reformed to my desire

Uptempo and thumping bass of the Funk
Soft, silky, smoothness of the Jazz
Uplifting, inspiring, triumph of the Spirituals
Just a sprinkle of the Classical

It's one way that I cope – with the daily issues I face
time bends around me - I control this world of thought
creation
The syncopation gives logic and comprehension to reality
Secrets of sound unlocks hidden potential that lift my
unrealized dreams,
which then move outward into the physical world
Dramatically my darkness is pierced by the lushness
of the sounds that fills my head
This therapy is primary auditory
but I can "see", "feel", "touch" the rhythmic vibrations
we define as Music

Still plugged in as the day comes to a close – it drives my
mood and becomes part on my
Rotation

MY THOUGHTS

Just sitting here thinking about you
How far we have come and what you mean to me
Life has many challenges and disappointments
I have had my share
The months and years have past and I was ashamed
Of what I had accomplished and where I was in life
My Mother has always prayed and helped me along the way
I love and am always grateful to her
But I leaned to my own understanding instead of being lead
by
The Spirit
The results were disastrous
Chasing after falseness
Not compatible
In the world
Then I come back to God
Found a beautiful Church and begin to make Christ a part
Of my daily life
The blessings have not ceased
I have gained peace of mind
My troubles don't seem so insurmountable
And most important, I have found the Love of God
And You
Thank you, Beloved

PAIN VISITED TODAY

Unwelcomed company came by to see me
today
We know him as Pain
Can't be seen but strongly felt
A succubus-draining my energy and
replacing it with his
Pain has my full attention-demanding
that I acknowledge his presence
Not only my body but he has my mind
thinking only of him
Pain is in total control-Can't stand it
Have asked him to leave several times
But he is the type that leaves when he is ready
I'm hurting, fighting against Pain
Can't get on with my day-it belongs to
him
Pleaded and begged but falls into
deafness
Crying out for help but no relief
Hearing Pain laugh because I am
powerless
As the day fades into night I hope
he decides to leave
Leave so I can become me again
But it seems it is all up to him..........
To decide when he is ready to
Leave................

PROGRESSION AND REGRESSION

Moving forward and making changes
-but the past tugs at the edges of my mind
Mind battles between clarity and confusion which
-leaves me barren and numb
Frustrated because I know where the help is
-available for me to tap into
Having the alien intellect to reason to
-logical outcomes to irrational situations
Words tumble out that make no sense compared to what
-the brain calculates
To one that I speak to has no idea of what is happening
- think I'm tripping
Started the day on the progressive
- thinking positive and looking to making my day joyous
I don't even understand the process so how can I explain it
to the person that wants to be involved
Progression pulls forward and Regression backwards
Need the balance of the opposites to
-keep my sanity intact
Know I'm not crazy but the grip is slipping
-slowly slipping

You Know You Can
Can You Know You?

PURPOSE OF

Words articulated

Feelings emancipated

Thoughts processed and ordered

Structure and logic

Hidden profound meanings

From deep in my soul

My purposeful process

of scribing

To share a part of me

So other's may "see"

Who and what I am

The essence

The truth

The spirit

Of what inspires me

To place words in the physical plane

RECTIFICATION

The evening last dissolved into blankness
Feelings of emptiness and questions
Floating
Frustration of not being heard
Searching and grasping for anything to gravitate to
and be solid
Overtaken by madness
Resentment fills the air
love for each other - yet
disconnected……
Rooted in our own ways
Standing at opposite sides of the situational room
Silence thick and Fear obstructs words from releasing
into the atmosphere
Not the calm of the sea at twilight
But the darkness and silence of the abyss

This needs to be rectified
I uproot myself like a seed off a flower
Not knowing where I will land
At the mercy of the wind
A move, a move is needed

To rectify
A new day begins
with the expectation of opportunity
at the rising of the sun
I make the choice to reconnect
To erase the blankness, the emptiness

The rectification
a renewed commitment
to see
to listen
to understand
to grow
to connect
to understand the meaning of why
Embracing the power of manhood
to seize the chance to give comfort to
my Beloved

SUPER SOUL

Working out preparing for the final life game
Training since I was young with various coaches
Parents, teachers and friends have taught me
Techniques to get me ready
Formed some bad habits that have set me back
The opposition has spied on my practices and know
Some of my signatures moves
For this ultimate game is played alone no one can
Substitute
Along the sidelines here is a coach that we hire if
We so choose
He has offered his advice as the season unfolds
Many winning records ignore and scoffs
Refusing to check his playbook
A few ask that he call the plays and allow them to
Execute
Over the years the chain moves first down
Sacked over the years but still in the game
Great effort is needed because no one knows when
The final whistle will sound
If a sound game plan is not in place you lose
But if you have it together and play hard
You win for eternity.

THE TIME

the distance is a hallway that extends beyond
doors on either side as I walk to the final place
i'm tempted to look into the unknown behind certain doors
but i know my destiny is at the end of the journey

the floor gives way beneath my feet
each breath i take is short making me want more
struggling to keep my mind on the task of moving forward
ever forward

arms reach out from the doors beckoning me to peer in
i hear sounds from within the doors
darkness from underneath the door jams
sounds of pleasure and pain
tugging at the edges of my mind
which is overcast and dreary
making my trip even harder

but i am drawn to the prize at the end of the hallway
the door will open to a bright outside
full of life and light
my focus needs to be like a ray piercing through the
darkness
the sounds are the noises of spring newness
so the rooms lose their power of persuasion over me
i pull away and keep moving
ever forward

TWO WORLDS
(I exist in both)

This dichotomy is my world
Mind's eye shut then opened
Shut I control the outcome of
my destiny
People love me with agape love
Feelings as a cornucopia of
a tasty and filling feast
For me to indulge to satisfy my desire
I'm mesmerized by how
colorful and real this place can be
Happy thoughts and joy dominate
as the movement of ideas flow
effortlessly
Thoroughly am I understood
Heard with clarity of ringing bells
CLEAR...................
Truly this is the world where I choose
to reside
THEN....................
My eyes open
The "real" world appears
And is thrusted upon me
No time to prepare
Everyone has a different attitude
Speaking I surmise clearly but
not heard
Hearing the spoken words that
I have no cognitive evidence of
uttering
Confusion, miscommunication has their
way in ruling this physical domain
Happiness, joy being sucked out and
dispatched to a place unreachable
I live thru my open eyes
Debating, compromising, devalued
for others enjoyment
I want to do what is right
Moving in step with the Word to apply
to this "world"
He gives peace to "eyes" closed to rest
and energize
Then the Spirit to walk with me
"eyes" Open

VISIONS OF ORDERED WORDS

Anticipation of the articulation

Manipulation of my thoughts to

oscillate in order and logic

Constant conflict against apathy

and despair when encountering

obstructions, distractions, manic

visions pulling toward insanity

A need to search out serenity in the

eye of tumultuous ideas which lure to

the pathway of hopelessness and desperation

Who declares that I am sane?

Does the culmination of all my moments

lead to the reality of now or the illusion as to

what is real?

Focusing on the illumination of the words I

choose to scribe matriculates to where I should be

Now my thoughts are structured and spontaneous,

revealing a true perception of me for you to review

WAKING UP

Moving through a world of dreams
Transforming from one region to another
Not being able connect how I arrived
Vivid colors blind my sight
I know this is not real, but I feel drawn in
Desiring to wake up but caught between realms
of sleep and wakefulness
Wanting to continue to the end of the surreal
But having to flow back to reality

My body feels tired and worn
is it all in my mind?
Am I being lead by what I am or the Spirit
that I asked to receive?

This is where sometimes a battle is waged
The enemy has penetrated my time of sleep
Peace escapes me as I search this imaginary world
that is real for the moment

Attempting to make meaning to bring back and use
when waking up
Then there is a loud buzzing sound
that shocks me back into the state of

Waking Up

WHEN I HAD NOTHING

Living in an empty space
Everything familiar changed for my lifetime
Family, friends faded into Nothing
Devoid of essentials folks take for granted

Frig and cabinets bare of
sustenance to feed my physical needs
Countless hours to reflect
on what I was missing or had

When I had Nothing

Noone could relate to my situation
Couldn't articulate my feelings
Too ashamed and afraid of the
reactions that would be aimed in my direction
Humbled physically, mentally and spiritually

Seeing the empty nothingness fueled
anger and embarrassment -
humiliation and pain
Mental space moved to depression and private despair
Smiling on the external while being crushed internally
spirit was put in place to reflect on
past deeds and choices made

When I had Nothing

Knowledge that there were others
much worse off than me
Feeling sorry for me - all alone
Lying to friends about how I was truly living
Closed part on who I was to the world
A decisive moment came to pass in this
time of reflection and introspection
A realization that I had more than Nothing
Beyond the physical I can process knowledge and
hope for the future

My Help had been waiting, waiting for me through this
whole ordeal, ordeal of cleansing
Purging my arrogance and ego
Steps taken to move pass the Nothingness
into the epiphany of what I always possessed
The gift of mind and soul I was blessed with
And the opportunity of what lies ahead

WORK OUT SPIRIT

Feeling a need to improve
the outer shell
Winter slumber has dulled the sinews from
inactivity
Craving that "high" after pushing to the edge
-such a long time ago
Seeing myself bare
-experiencing the pains of age
-like a door that hasn't been opened in years
Effort to move those rusted hinges,
creaking and eventually giving way to the
sustained force of commitment
Bringing into harmony
body and mind
physical and mental
flesh and inner spirit
Liken to a seedling planted and covered
by earthly soil
By force it survives the elements and
produces a strong and rigid tree
which extends skyward pointing to a higher
purpose
A majesty that endures and thrives through time
This is what I seek
Working my body into summer richness
To draw in the radiance of the sun
and polish this shell to a bright luminous glow
Balance is the intricate and vital piece to this
rotation
The "inner" body needs to play a part in this sacrament
Body and Spirit are truly "One" for total peace and harmony of
life
This is my mantra that moves and motivates
my dual existence
Strengthening the body for endurance
Work the Spirit by exercising the Word
Physical movement changes the outer frame
The weight that the Word brings will
get your Spirit body in "shape"
What an "afterglow" I feel
as the cooldown begins

YOU

You bring me so much joy
To hear in your voice how you feel about me
Not having seen or heard from you since my youth
Hearing you telling me how handsome I am and how much
you
Appreciate our rekindled friendship
Words cannot truly express what I feel
I'm just putting words together because of what I'm feeling

Damn, I'm so happy
I feel it ever so strongly
My spirit is soaring
The sky is clear and blue
The sun is shining so brightly
And the biggest thing that it is because of who you are

Thank you for being who you are
Thank you for living the life that brings you to me now
Thank you for the emotional context you bring with your
words and thoughts

The pouring out of my heart is so freeing
I have NEVER felt like this before
I truly do need you
I do want you-but all in time

This should move you to great things
PEACE and LOVE!

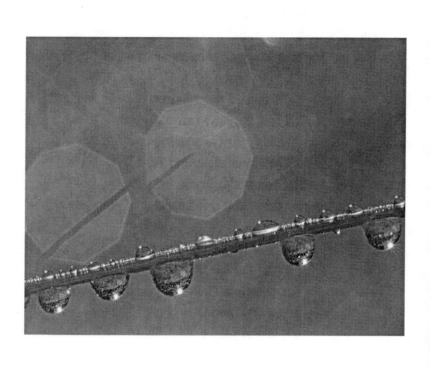

3rd

R O T A T I O N

OBSERVATIONAL

WHERE ARE THE BROTHERS?

Sitting here listening to the Word being recited
Excitement resonates as the anticipation pulls my thoughts to
reflect on my journey
The Spirit fills me and I rock with the rhythm of a pendulum
Back and forth – Forth and Back
A calm feeling hugs me and gives me peace
I am sitting..............................alone

Where are the Brothers?

The congregation is small, intimate
But the persuasion are the Sisters whose numbers drive the
service
Representing the desire to come out and serve
Sisters represent a strong and powerful force
We move up and down in our numbers
At times standing joined together –
tonight diminished and quiet
We need to make a loud noise in the house by being here

Our presence is required to balance the flow of the vision
Our strength is needed to fulfill the role intended
Our commitment is vital - the momentum to push forward the
purpose we share

To move to a level where we can share in what the Lord has
intended, our presence is required
for our growth as members of this tree of life
A tree cannot grow and bear fruit without the proper root
foundation which we Brothers represent
Even with rain growth is stunted and slow - branches that are
weak are not capable of dealing with reaching upward and
outward to provide comfort and shade for the community we
serve

Each one must look separately at themselves in order to come
together
Desire must be in place to want to fulfill the role that we are
commanded to take by the
Father
Being accountable to each other as Christian Brothers

Where are the Brothers?

A Few Days

So many differences in us
How we think, see, articulate
Opinions clear the net
Your forehand to my backhand
Mind games moved to reality
You hear red and I blue
Both colors but not the same
Like a hammer to a brick wall
It has to come down
For freedom and joining together
Not mad, just flustered
Flapping and fluttering around aimlessly
Looking for the purpose of it all
Feels like speaking in a empty room-
full of myself
Holding on to the hope and sight of
a new day
Build a sand castle over a few days
Desire to know you like me
Do you? Like me?
So we can hold hands and stroll
the beach of contentment
Leaving behind us, the wall of separation
that we have crumbled, and left as
granules of sand beneath our feet
Giving us courage for a few days

CHANGE

seasons cycle with the heavens
day fades into night
relationships transition into a life
of their own
warmth becomes cold and icy
distance and creepy
no understanding as to why
is it cause and effect?
or the individuals choice to

Change

i long for stability
the daily rising of the sun
stars in the sky at night
even behind the clouds
a steady and comfortable

Change

not the volatile temperament
that people exhibit
have I become different as well?
moved from a place where I was?
i question and search for an answer
know what i'm feeling at this very moment
like waves rushing in and out from the shore
of our many beaches
leaving and returning but not the same each time

Change

will happen and this i accept
but not when it is devoid and empty of the
connection we as people should share with
one another

CLEAR SIGHTING

road unfolds
Rises and falls like
the movement of my chest
Smooth and winding
left and rights
In sync-pumping arms
Strides stretching out
Squirrels darting across the path
Sunlight cuts thru the canopy of trees
Light dancing in and out
from the shadows of the afternoon
Senses extending outward
Floral fragrances interrupt each breath
i take
Chirping snaps my head to and fro
Looking forward to keep the focal point
from running away
Air comes to hang out and cools me
Sweat pours from the exertion of my body
Sighting inward and outward
A mind quest has been started for me to complete
The body must join to reach the goal and appease
the buzzing around my head
Aching in my legs feels like ground crying for
rain when dry
Hard breathing-need a strong breeze to refresh
the air
Clear sighting
To reach the end
Pushing up the strength in me-pines and oaks
stand at attention saluting me
To be satisfied reaching my rank in the natural order

Cloudy Rainy Day

Existing at my desk working thru this dreary day
I say that because looking out the window that's all

I see

Overcast, raindrops-grey and foreboding
Limbs - slaves to the "massa" wind
Sun discriminated against
Locked away and forgotten for this day
Dragging work like a cross - mental weights
hurting my thinking

Stuck in a box and can't escape
E-mails non-stop with demands that are non-negotiable
To survive I must succumb
A reality as real as truth

But then before the quicksand of routine can suck me in
A hand of hope reaches in and pulls me free
Not really surprised because it is always there

Advising not to wander to the despair and sadness of now
But to visualize the brightness of tomorrow-
For I know and believe that the cloudy rainy day -
Will surrender and be conquered by the
Sunny Bright Day (selah)

INADMISSIBLE

Court is in session
Jury eyes fixed on the sins of the defendant
A plea is needed to reduce the judge's sentence
Evidence planted and the frame is on
Who are the ones that sit in judgment?
Bias enters into the proceedings
Race, culture and economic raiment
force us to choose
Guilt or innocence
Our peers convict us
They don't want to serve
Scales of justice out of balance
Worldly system corrupt to its rotten core
Pure ideas, evil agendas
Someone plead guilty on our behalf
Sentenced and convicted
Double jeopardy
Acquitted and released
Be grateful and cherish the freedom
Or forfeit and be brought back where
the charges and evidence will be
admissible

EDGE

Rough under the soles of my feet
Peering downward spins my mind like a
amusement park ride
Fro or back?

Life brought me here and left
Where do I look for knowledge or wisdom?
Can't go ahead, will plunge into the unknown- I'm scared
Not going to the past-left her behind

The riddle of the dilemma
A smile cracks of the face of the sphinx
Answer wrong results in death

Will the correct utterance lead to an alternative plane?
A way to escape from where I am?
Or is it all in my head?

FRINGE *(dreaming in the day)*

Sitting here dreaming in the
day
Thoughts drifting and swirling around this
moment
About visionary things - far off but can still be
seen
Being carried by the flow of my
being
Allowing myself to let
go
Not holding
on
Free floating in
time
Serene, no effort or resistance to create friction to hinder
me
Body and spirit intermingle to create an alternate
reality
To dwell here is paradise in the
moment
Searching for the secret to capture and
snare
time, moment and feelings to shape it into what I need and
desire

To control that power will be wonderful-
Tapping into that source whenever I want
Sharing outwardly with anyone who has the sight
For so many are blind - Others are asleep
For me as I curl up
Wrap my arms around this
Blissful, wonderful releasing energy that sustains,
Maintains and entertains

Friendship Dies

You told me even though things didn't work out
we could still be friends
But you have not forgiven me for how it ended
anger seethes and rises within you
Your words sting and your silence confirms it

The path I'm attempting to take is difficult
knocking on a door that may never be opened
waiting for an answer but receiving the echoes of
nothingness
living in the world and moving toward the Word
I hear whispers for me to stand and wait
with the patience of a great oak
or choosing to just walk away and put distance
and time in its place
But if I am to truly live what I am fed,
I must make amends

As the seasons unfold, winter brings slumber to
the things of spring
But the seasons cycle as I wait for spring to come
hoping that we renew ourselves
Me not wanting our friendship to die
but wanting our place we have been to blossom into
something different and new

Would your heart open to feed the soil of forgiveness?
Or will the shade and dryness of the mind make the earth
barren?

KNIGHTS OF POOL

A gathering takes place
Brothers in Arms
To do battle royale on the field of
confrontation
Friendly but spirited verbal
exchanges
Mahogany, cedar, pine lances
Our weapons we brandish
skillfully
Balls scatter after the attack
on the break
One by one we call where the
enemy will be vanquished into the pockets
of the abyss
Each Knight displays his strategy and
cunning
Battle cries are uttered by a few
Bold words claiming victory before
the game is concluded and the outcome
determined
When the game is lost a place is reserved
for the loser
Taunted and humiliated they must lie in wait
for another chance
To annihilate each foe to obtain
"the crown"
Seven victories must be achieved
to be coroneted
"King of Pool Knight"

MY STATE OF BEING

The newness of our re-acquaintance
Has been like a breathe of fresh air
The feeling of a deep sleep and suddenly
Awakening from hibernation into Spring
From moment to moment
I flow into the beauty that has moved from
How are You, to My Beloved I miss you …..
The reality of my emotions have become clouded
By the distance that binds us
It's difficult to collect my thoughts
As they get tossed into the mixture of'
Love, Darkness, Contention, Sunshine, and Rain
I hold onto what is real for me
In this moment of time
For this is all I have
Until this mountain has been moved……
I wrestle with the thoughts of
Creating a new life, a future
The picture I've painted
On floating billowy clouds,
It seems so clear….
And here I stand
Eyes wide open to the view
Of what is real, my inability to
Feel you, touch you, BE-IN-TO-YOU
This is all that remains of my imagined artistry
Until the state of my being, becomes being with you.

LOGIC OF THE IRRATIONAL

Conversation behind the wheel
A quick shot to wake up
to make the dull drive tolerable
Love the technology-to talk with
no hands
Throwing sentences in the atmosphere
to be heard and acknowledged
Playing word tennis-I serve, she volleys
Points not scored yet
Not keeping track-just enjoying playing

In my mind-logic is cool
Arrived where I was headed
Prepared for the day of work
A feeling hits - reach out to share what's in
my head
Can't call so I text-love the technology
Logic says I should hear something soon

Time and work join and I'm in the loop
Flip to irrational-no answer
Why is that? the message was important
and from the heart
But should it been spoken?

Is technology flawed?
Or user error?
Where is the logic in that?

LISTENING "IN-SIGHT"

"Outside" myself
I listen thru you to understand me
I take her place and listen
With her hearing as I speak
We talk of many things you're feeling.........
I "hear" myself giving wisdom
from the knowledge I assume I possess
You hear
"He wants me to do......."
"Only what is right in His mind"
"His perspective is absolute"
"Talking all over what I have to say"
Not giving you a chance to put thoughts in the mix

The guard goes Up
I feel her defense is now turned on and way up
The volume is pushed to LOUD
Her mind screams
"YOU ARE NOT HEARING ME"
Through it all she says the love is always there
That this moment won't change
How she feels for Me
But in the midst thoughts move to....
an isolated and dark place.....
Disconnected and shallow....
Anger grows in her
because I believe that My talk
is good for both for us
But she hears what is perceived as
My boldness and arrogance
a wave that will wash over her
And move her to My way of thinking
because of who I think I am
She is grounded and
"WILL BE HEARD AND
ACKNOWLEDGED"
i now flow back into me
listening now with a renewed
sense of what is really happening
we are growing into a newness with one another
learning and moving thru
loud thoughts and then silence
trying to rise above it all
But having life chains
that keeps us bound
i now know how i sound to you
i commit myself to truly
hearing you with "in-sight-fullness"
by listening thru YOU
compels me to hear what i'm saying

STROLLING IN THE MIDST

Words to understand and live
Cut to the soul and breathe
Inhaling the conviction and sure
sentence of damnation
Knowledge pulsates with each passage
Time dissolves and fades
Thoughts unable to embrace the vastness
To which there are no known limits
Faith underfoot
Wrap up in truth to keep out the
Coldness of this world
Fear approaches – begging for a place
Voices in the distance
Speak beyond what Is seen
Trust when you walk if you are being told
The truth
Lies feel so smooth and easy to embrace
Truth waits alone at the narrow path
Speaking some cannot hear
Looking others cannot see
Existence in deaf darkness
Reach not with your hands
But with spirit, heart and yes – your soul

The Door

Ornate design.
Mahogany wood.
Brass polished handle.
Smooth to the touch.
Heavy and fixed on its frame.

We stand before it to make a choice.
Enter or gaze.
Reach or hesitate at the appointed moment.
We each will reach The Door.

What lies beyond is a mystery many do not
contemplate.
Never in ones thoughts because the significance has
been diminished.

For the chosen who have opened and stepped through
questions have been answered,
emotions galvanized,
emptiness filled.

For this Door is the entrance to your soul and what
lies beyond this physical domain.

THE SMELL OF THE AIR AFTER THE RAIN

Seems like the raindrops are angry with me
Constant pounding against my skin
The wetness doesn't feel friendly at all
Mixing with my tears

Wanting the outcome to be something else
But acknowledging that it must rain to clean the air
A spiritual filter to purify and prepare
The clouds are parted by invisible hands

The air is light and carries life within
As I breathe my soul is renewed and refreshed
Because I sense that the rain was meant for me
To give me hope and new understanding of things
above and below.....................

YESTERDAY LOST

Reaching back to emptiness
Memories faded to forgetfulness
Building on nothing
Actions guided by flesh and not
Remembered
Emotions sucked out and crushed into dust
Imagination at work
False images as to what yesterday was
Time never reverses
Words spoken cannot be withdrawn
Moments disappear and evaporate
Desires want to influence and
Correct
What is lost cannot be brought back – so
Today is a gift
To make amends and forgive
Needing to embrace the newness of
Tomorrow

YOU PAY

Who do you owe?
Folks have given their time to advise
for better or worse
Was the debt ignored or paid in full?
When you heard the ringing, did you answer?
You know the debt is owed

People coming to collect
Is there enough in your account to cover?
One way or another the payment will be
settled

Some have been forgiven, agreements have
been singed
Voluntarily or under duress

There's that ringing again-hope you aren't
afraid to pick it up

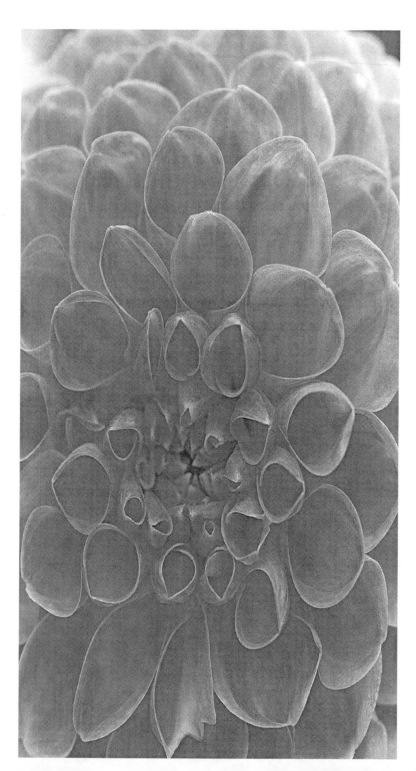

4th
ROTATION

RELATIONSHIPS

a need to fulfill

My intention is to help
in a time of need
But being mindful
of the twists and turns
of what that means
Is it for the virtue of
others or myself
Am I being used and
not aware?
Searching for the place
in my core which will
warn and make me
conscious of a myriad
of choices
Guarding the emotions
that are a part of me
Pleading and making
its case to influence me
Words and intentions
are tossed about
Have I been given the
wisdom to know the
difference?
Learning that being
unconditional in reaching
out is the true way
Because the reward
has been promised
But I don't want to play
the role of the fool in
life's stage play
A need to fulfill will be
revealed............
I
Am
Preparing
Me

A "PSALMIC" VERSE

She loveth from her heart to please the Father
Knoweth the role and power bequeathed
Embraces beauty from within and adores herself with
humility
Speaks words of wisdom and listens with an ear of
understanding
Encourages one to reach for the heavens
Places a boldness to take on whatever lies ahead
Peers inward with a vision that transcends what is common

Her inward spirit radiates outward and warms like the sun
Bright and blinding is her goodness
Power of influence is the talent she has been given
Skilled as a warrior marching into battle
But with softness of lamb's wool

The Father has placed her for a helpmeet
Companion to walk on this road to an uncertain future
Fortified with her strength I stand tall-her love sustains
and fills
A pure love that does not waver
For that is the reason that the Father-in His infinite
wisdom
Man and creation was not complete-
Without her by his side-to share and to love

A STAND

Made a stand for me
Refused to take the abuse
Rising in my strength

Told them how I felt
Would not be treated that way
I hope they get it

If not I will leave
The friendship will end
A Stand must be made

COOL NIGHT SKY

As I gaze into the heavens I think of you
This simple sky is that rich midnight blue sprinkled
with the white specks of light
The moon burns its luminance
onto my upward countenance
Overwhelmed with the vastness of the space above

Endless possibilities of the future that we want to share
Riding on the wave of meteors from galaxy to galaxy
Starlight reaching me tonight that started thousands
of years before-just reaching me at
this precise moment in the time criterion
No need to understand the science of this-just take in the
natural beauty of what God has created
So much that we don't need to understand or analyze
Love is the common band like the lines that join the
constellations
Just listen to the sky - it is silent yet speaks to the heart of
my being

As I gaze to the heavens I think of you
My senses are vibrant-seeing eyes, touching air, smelling at
the night sky, hearing the quiet of space, feeling
your heart
It's truly that easy for me
No need to have the knowledge of why
The beauty is just to accept that it is-thoughts that pass
beyond our understanding
My heart tells me to simply-
Love you as much as I see when I look into the heavens

DISTANCE WARFARE

We gazed at each other from across the lands
Desire danced in our hearts
Yearning to be loved up close

But the Distance proclaims
"You must defeat me first"
Courage and strength must be found to prepare for this
Uncertainty is an inconvenience, I reason with myself to
stay in control

I rally my army to stand with me
Anxiety leads to the doorway of doubt to penetrate my
defenses
My feelings are solidified
The quest is set

to prepare myself and my army for battle
The Distance and his minions stand against me
For the war I have pledged to fight, the cause is true

Though spies have infiltrated my ranks
I am not confused, fear spreads thru the camp
Loudly I speak to fortify those who follow me

The battle will continue, for it wages on
Until Distance is defeated and banished from the land

FACE MASK

What lies behind?
I thought I knew
How is it different?
You act like I'm a stranger
Is it for good or evil?
One moment changed it all
Why was the mask removed?
A friendship might be dissolved
Were we ever friends at all?
Makes me wonder why you have one
Is there a need to hide what's inside?
There is a reason which needs to be revealed
But is it a lie or your true nature?
I really would like to talk it out
Why is it so cold around you?
I have seen the transformation
Are we friends or adversaries?
Didn't know you were wearing a mask around me
So what is the truth of the matter?
Hard to comprehend if I ever knew you
Any reason for you misleading me?
Or maybe it's just how you are
Is this how I must deal with everyone?
Looking for the mask and not beyond
Are you ever going to share?
Who you truly are

FACES

Thought I knew you
We spent time together
I felt I loved you

And you said you loved me
What happened?
You said it wasn't me
I truly miss you so much
But you asked that I don't reach out to you
Each day I get better
But do I really want to?
You showed me different
FACES
Were they real?
I feel they were
Maybe one day you will share with me
YOUR
TRUE
FACE

IN THE MOMENT

Just to join you in this place

Enhances the life current in me

Being of one mind even though we

Are apart

Is a joy that cannot be explained

It can only be felt by the participants

In the moment

Treasured and significant because it

Will end someday

Need to embrace and sense the beauty

In the moment

Funny that it can only be shared with one

In the moment……..

JOURNEY

As I sit here and contemplate
I basically need to elaborate

All of the things we have gone through since we met
And at no time did I regret

The vibe and conversations that we have shared
What we have risked and dared

To take a chance to recapture something we had a long time
ago
Are we willing to give it a go?

We have grown so much spiritually
And connect so continuously

My love grows for you day by day
Is there anything more that I can say?

The future looks bright with the possibilities and God's
Hand
So let's you and I make a stand

To work together to make this a reality
Making it stronger by the clarity

Of our commitment and love
Like the rising of the dove

Of Peace, Harmony and Strength
May we be blessed with a longer life length

To be able to love as we have spoken
Be with each other and never be broken

That is my desire for this day and going forward

LIFE RHYTHM

Thoughts harmonic
Major or minor keys
Resonating in our heads
Soft as smooth jazz
or hard as heavy metal
We all move to the music of
our existence
Let's float on the sound waves
thru the difficult stanzas
Some of you will choose to turn the music
off
Many will constantly change the beat
and tinker with the rhythm
Spend your life searching,
reaching for the rhythm that gives
meaning and balance to what sounds
and feels right to you
Can we create a rhythm that will leave a
legacy?
Or will not a single soul remember our
life song

MANDINGO

Not a stud
A majestic warrior
Of African descent
Strong and proud
Free never bound
Fearless and protective
A name bestowed
By my beloved
To describe me
A Black man
In her world
I am honored
To represent this
For it is
What I am
In her eyes

LOOKING BETWEEN TWO
(A POETIC CONVERSATION)

LOOKING THRU

Man, we different beasts
Not looking to the east
Do we try to be "into" one another?
Or just working undercover
We call each other Beloved
But when we talk, we push and shove
You say you reach out and share because of
your concerns
But a lot of those things, I don't need to learn
Gotta get on the same page
If we are going to be together and age
Claiming praying for insight and wisdom
Man we looking thru a different prism
Need to wake up and pay attention
Or constantly upping the tension
Making me feel that we don't need to talk
Enemy whispering for me to walk
I'm in this for the long haul
But sometime you say I have a lot of gall
Each of us have things to improve
Then things would run smooth
So as you read these lines, take the time today
To think so we won't go astray

■

LOOKING BACK

*You say you feel like we are not on the same page
When I speak, there are things you'd rather I didn't say
We are different beasts this is true
I am ME and YOU are YOU*

*I have uncovered myself slowly to reveal who I am
A woman of strength, courage and spirit is where I stand
When I give I do so from within, there is nothing hidden in
the sand
You say think about the lines you've penned in your scribe
I say look at what has been given to you and really decide
If you have given all that you can, to make this
relationship continue to stand*

*You know of the challenges that we face, what have you
done to stay in this race
Against time that we live with day in and day out, the
fight to keep the devil out
Of what we SAY God has blessed us with, Are we truly His
Gift?
I try to understand what my place is in this partnership
At times no matter what I do there seems to be a rift
One thing I do know for sure, There is a God and He will
lead me
Thru the right door that reveals a Path that two can
journey upon
Question is will we find one another at the crossroads that
join?*

*Here I stand after a year, further along than before
But still haunted by old responsibilities that stand in the
way on new opportunities
What is the possibility that moving forward means
movement and not just the
Thought of what that could be? Here I stand in the midst
of I wonder, how soon,
When will, I hope, If, maybe, Damn........ But yet here I
stand, shouldn't that account for something?*

Think about that
by Vernesa

∎

TURNED AROUND

See you want reply with a scribe
That's kool so then we can vibe
You are all the things you say
And with none of that will I play
But I also have grown and contributed
My feelings distributed
Honest and free-holding back nothing
That has to count for something
You have and take credit for what you feel
you have done
Not a game like you have won
Look inward have I
And upward to the sky
Prayed and cried to stay strong and keep the
relationship real
So coming back like that, what's the deal?
Telling me to think about that
Do you feel I'm really that whack?
With no idea how to handle a partnership
I definitely have a grip
Blunt and harsh I may sound
But I'm grounded and profound
Just trying to give a different perspective
Be open and bit more reflective
You told know where you came from
Heard and I am done
This is new and different
Hopefully more proficient
So release your inner self
And do me like you do yourself ■

EYE TO EYE

Sometimes I truly wonder if you really see
The depth of who I am as a woman indeed
Your growth has not been denied nor has it
been pushed aside
But you must understand true growth doesn't
come today then go away
Yes you have shared yourself from the surface
to the core and
Wondered at the same time can she take much more?
Not because I have
Held up a stop light or cut you off but because the things
you bring sometimes trip you up!!
I do not need accolades for any deeds, nor
am I waiting to be crowned
The things you don't see, my tears, my fears, frustration
the way my heart pounds
When I am lonely and needing you and you
are not there, to the heavens
I reach, my Savior he's there, he knows and he tells me
my child be still
Continue to worship me and do my will)
I have said this once and I'll say it again my time on
this earth I shall not waste
I'm keeping it real with you I'm sure you can relate
to the realness I share
No need to debate, You know what it is, so let's Stop
and contemplate
What is needed to move with movement, so that we can see
All that this relationship is supposed to be.
We can do one of two things as I see it now
Talk about it or Be about it the work Is In HOW!
So no blows, no punches below the belt
All that's inside has been released
Take it and use it to step with a plan
That's my expectation…. Because you're my MAN!!!!■
by Vernesa

108

AWAKENED TO A DREAM

Escape to a mind making scene

Can't deal with reality at the moment

Slapped to the brink of unconsciousness

Aware of fantasy rising from nothingness

Manifested by mere thought

A world shaped by my desires

Pulling at the same time

But in different directions

Seeking peaceful slumber

Realness pierces thru the

Artificial sky

Rain from a nightmarish storm

Raging dark winds

Flooding inner clarity

Cause to Reason

Strolling thru taking in the sights
So much to take in but time is edgy
Twisting and turning to comprehend
Still confused-knowing nothing
Ignorance swells, the fragrance of
understanding creeps into the recesses
of mind

Chaotic sky's thunder and moment lightning
strikes
Not wanting to get wet search for shelter
Pounding drops to insane roar giving cause
to take medication
So artificial but real
Where is the line drawn between worlds?
Don't they blur into one

Questions to be pondered
One by one, day by day
Reasoning will culminate into answers
at some point
But in the meantime head moving side
to side wanting to see and smell
sense

ROSES AND WINE
(kudos Iris Yanette Seda)

Your garden is in

bloom

When I visit my senses are heightened by

the sweet smell of your words

I then sample your special vintage wine that

you have prepared

As I sip, the message caresses my tongue

as it goes down ever so smoothly

Smells and tastes to marinate on sitting in the

vineyard-soothed by the warmth of the afternoon sun

Continue to grow your roses and the grapes

for your wine to share with us all......

Season of Beloved

Exhale
the time is now
Alone
waiting for this Season to
finally arrive
Shedding the stiffness of
winter to hug and kiss the
Sun
She is the warmth and the
brightness
that melts and vanquishes the
cold
Feeling her embrace like the
cool evening breeze
Soothing and refreshing to my
soul
Curves as clouds riding the
horizon of sunset undulating
across the sky
Smiles from a countenance
beaming as the full moon on
a wonderful summer night
This is the
Season of Beloved
Weathered storms
of others who wanted to
break my spirit
Said that I would never
be in Season of happiness
Prophesied doom and
destruction of my world
Sowing the seeds of faith
and patience prepared me
to receive her
I pray that this Season lasts
for the harvest of my love and
life
For I am now reaping in the
Season of Beloved

SPACE BETWEEN EUPHORIC LONGING

Space
An invisible piece of the
universe
which applies directly to
me
Space for me is defined as the
miles
between me and my
beloved
Money would cause the distance to
disappear
Reaching out over the
frequencies
of airspace to hear her
voice
But that doesn't ease my
longing
to be in her
Space
Empty gaps-I miss
her
Attempts to busy space with
activity
to condense and minimize into
small
manageable
clusters

Space......so wide
Trying to cross to reach ......
Throw up my hands to rail against......

Who?
As each day passes I contemplate how to
implode
space into nothingness
So I can be with the one who I need to embrace
in mutual existence
without having
Space   separating   our   physical   bodies

ABOUT THE AUTHOR

Born in the Bronx, NY. Relocated to Atlanta in 1995. Attended SUNY College at Old Westbury. He has been inspired by his life's journey to come home to the spiritual place that he left a long time ago. He started writing poetry about two and a half years ago. He had no clue that this would be something he would have gotten into, but it feels right.

CPSIA information can be obtained at www.ICGtesting.com
Printed in the USA
LVOW070925220213

321230LV00001B/6/P

9 780984 037933